In the words of Nelson Mandela

A Little Pocketbook

Edited by Jennifer Crwys-Williams

PENGUIN BOOKS

PENGUIN BOOKS

Published by the Penguin Group
27 Wrights Lane, London W8 5TZ, England
Viking Penguin, a division of Penguin Books USA Inc,
375 Hudson Street, New York, New York 10014, USA
Penguin Books Australia Ltd, Ringwood, Victoria, Australia
Penguin Books Canada Ltd, 10 Alcorn Avenue, Toronto, Ontario,
Canada M4V 3B2
Penguin Books (NZ) Ltd, 182-190 Wairau Road, Auckland 10,
New Zealand
Penguin Books (South Africa) (Pty) Ltd, 1A Eton Road,
Parktown, South Africa 2193

Penguin Books (South Africa) (Pty) Ltd, Registered Offices:
1A Eton Road, Parktown, South Africa 2193

First published by Penguin Books 1997

Copyright © Jennifer Crwys-Williams 1997

ISBN 0 140 27049 3

Typeset in 11 on 13 pt Joanna
Printed and bound by The Rustica Press, Old Mill Rd, Ndabeni

This book is dedicated to the children of South Africa in the hope that as they grow they may find inspiration from the thoughts of Nelson Rolihlahla Mandela – and that, in his words on receiving the Nobel Peace Prize, they and other children the world over, may 'play in the open veld, no longer tortured by the pangs of hunger or ravaged by disease or threatened with the scourge of ignorance, molestation and abuse . . . Children are the greatest of our treasures.'

In particular, it is for the children in my own family, living in both the old and the new worlds: Amber, Cassandra, Sebastian and Phoebe.

Acknowledgements

Without the help of the marvellous Susan Segar, political correspondent of the *Natal Witness*, this book, quite literally, would not have been completed. It is rare to find a researcher who so completely understands what is needed that virtually everything that is wanted is used – as it was in this case.

Many thanks to Solly Masolo for helping me with research. My thanks too to Jill van Zyl and to the boffins who helped create (and run) the ANC home page (http://www.anc.org.za). As always, Nancy Ncube's generosity of spirit went beyond the normal confines of friendship.

My agent, Carole Blake of Blake Friedmann & Associates, and the staff of that company, have encouraged me with their enthusiasm. Rowland White of Michael Joseph has been a supportive and sensitive editor, and one with nerves of steel.

My special thanks to all the journalists who, over the years, have interviewed Nelson Mandela with skill and with passion, and who have provided me with much of the material used in this book. In particular, my thanks to the foreign correspondents, past and present, who helped me enormously.

The editor and publisher would like to thank the following for permission to quote from copyright material:

Fatima Meer, *Higher than Hope*, Penguin, 1990;

Patti Waldmeir, *Anatomy of a Miracle*, Viking, 1997.

Introduction

It is the fate of very few human beings to transcend the limits of their national boundaries and to become the property of the world. As this turbulent century and the millennium in which it finds itself draw to an end, the shadow cast by the slight figure of India's Mahatma Gandhi has touched virtually every nation on earth, as has that of Martin Luther King, Jnr. Both fought for the freedom of their own oppressed people, and in doing so fought for the freedom and dignity of people in far-flung lands, for freedom, dignity and hunger know no national boundaries.

So, too, has the almost messianic figure of South Africa's Nelson Rolihlahla Mandela stretched out to capture the hearts and the imaginations of the world's teeming peoples. How ironic that two of these men — the Mahatma and Mandela, should have intimately known the soil of the beloved country — South Africa — and have been affected by its sweeping beauty, its grandeur, its turbulent history and its racial prejudices in similar ways.

Was it just coincidence that all three men lit beacons which flamed across the world as they preached, sometimes with breathtaking courage and with a stubborn disregard for the personal consequences their message might bring, the credo of non-racialism? How ironic it was that Martin Luther King, Jnr's 'I Have a Dream' speech, which ended with 'Free at last! Free at last! Thank God almighty, we are free at last!', should have been made as Nelson Mandela was one year into his twenty-seven years' incarceration – and that Nelson Mandela should have uttered those selfsame words in 1994 as he cast his vote in South Africa's first democratic election.

Known to his countrymen and women as Madiba, Nelson Mandela is the world's role model. A towering figure of strength and forgiveness, he has been able to do the almost impossible: unite the bitterly divided people of the country of his birth. In so doing, he has been taken to the heart of both the mighty and the dispossessed the world over.

Nelson Mandela, whilst remaining a South African to the last fibre of his being, belongs to everyone, irrespective of where they live and, importantly for him, how they live. He has become, in the few years since his release from imprisonment, a symbol of reconciliation and, in a world divided by sectarian hatreds, a symbol of love.

He would protest: he avers that he is no saint — but to South Africans, Nelson Mandela's rainbow people, he has, quite simply, no parallel.

And perhaps his thoughts, reproduced on these pages, and honed over many years of tribulation and anguish, will inspire people, young and old, moneyed and impoverished, the world over. In particular, I hope it will inspire people who have had few role models in their lives, who have suffered their own apartheids in their own countries: there is light, there is hope and, above all, there is reconciliation.

Jennifer Crwys-Williams

On Abortion

Women have the right to decide what they
want to do with their bodies.

On Africa

The peoples of resurgent Africa are perfectly
capable of deciding upon their own future
form of government and discovering and
themselves dealing with any dangers which
might arise.

Africa, more than any other continent, has had
to contend with the consequences of conquest
in a denial of its own role in history, including
the denial that its people had the capacity to
bring about change and progress.

For centuries, an ancient continent has bled
from many gaping sword wounds.

No doubt Africa's renaissance is at hand — and our challenge is to steer the continent through the tide of history.

The people of the continent are eager and willing to be among the very best in all areas of endeavour.

We need to exert ourselves that much more, and break out of the vicious cycle of dependence imposed on us by the financially powerful: those in command of immense market power and those who dare to fashion the world in their own image.

It would be a cruel irony of history if Africa's actions to regenerate the continent were to unleash a new scramble for Africa which, like that of the nineteenth century, plundered the continent's wealth and left it once more the poorer.

On Being an African

Teach the children that Africans are not one iota inferior to Europeans.

From his seminal 'No Easy Walk to Freedom' address, 21 August 1953.

The lack of human dignity experienced by Africans is the direct result of the policy of white supremacy.

Spoken from the dock at the Rivonia Treason Trial, 20 April 1964, which sent him to prison for twenty-seven long years.

All of us, descendants of Africa, know only too well that racism demeans the victims and dehumanizes its perpetrators.

On the African National Congress

As no man is an island, so too are we not men of stone who are unmoved by the noble passions of love, friendship and human compassion.

He was referring to the formation of the ANC Youth League on Easter Sunday, 1944. Mandela and his lifelong friends Oliver Tambo and Walter Sisulu were prominent among its founding fathers — the young Turks of their day.

We must move from the position of a resistance movement to one of builders.

For us the struggle against racism has assumed the proportions of a crusade.

The African National Congress is the greatest achievement of the twentieth century.

From an interview in 1997, the year he relinquished his presidency of the party.

Human rights and the attainment of justice have explicitly been at the centre of our concerns.

On *Afrikaners*

As those who drew benefits from a previous programme of affirmative action, they should realize better than anyone else how such a programme can contribute towards making the community more productive.

I have often noticed Afrikaans people remark that the new South Africa gives them a feeling of freedom now that they have entered a wider world of relationships with fellow South Africans.

The challenge of the New Patriotism is not one of a choice between Afrikanerdom and being South African. On the contrary, it is precisely about the healing reconciliation of Afrikaners with being fully South African.

Maybe it was out of fear that they themselves would one day become the oppressed once again.

On possible reasons for the Afrikaners oppressing fellow South Africans during apartheid, and spoken in the tense run-up to South Africa's first democratic elections in 1994.

On Age

What nature has decreed should not generate undue insecurity.

I am nearing my end. I want to be able to sleep until eternity with a broad smile on my face, knowing that the youth, opinion-makers

and everybody is stretched across the divide,
trying to unite the nation.

*From a speech to students at the University of Potchefstroom, February
1996. He was seventy-seven; Nelson Mandela was born in the tiny
Transkei village of Mvezo on 18 July 1918.*

On Alliances

No true alliance can be built on the shifting
sands of evasions, illusions and opportunism.

On Anger

Anger is a temporary feeling – you soon
forget it, particularly if you are involved in
positive activities and attitudes.

It is not easy to remain bitter if one is busy
with constructive things.

On Apartheid

Apartheid is the rule of the gun and the hangman.

Apartheid itself was a war against the people.

The universal struggle against apartheid was not an act of charity arising out of pity for our people, but an affirmation of our common humanity.

Out of the experience of an extraordinary human disaster that lasted too long, must be born a society of which all humanity will be proud.

At his inauguration as President of South Africa, 10 May 1994.

It would have been immoral to keep quiet while a racist tyranny sought to reduce an entire people into a status worse than that of beasts of the forest.

The millions of graves strewn across Europe which are the result of the tyranny of Nazism, the decimation of the native peoples of the

Americas and Australia, the destructive trail of the apartheid regime against humanity — all these are like a haunting question that floats in the wind: why did we allow these to happen?

Bill of Rights

A Bill of Rights is an important statement about the nature of power relations in any society.

The ANC has had a Bill of Rights since 1923.

A Bill of Rights cannot be associated with the political or economic subordination of either the majority or the minority.

On South African Blacks

The blacks think this transformation was brought about by military victory, and they have defeated the whites. They think the whites are lying on the floor and begging for mercy.

From an interview during his July 1996 state visit to the United Kingdom.

On Bosnia

They [the leaders] thought through their blood and not through their brains.

On Boxing

Any boxer with skill I admire.

Nelson Mandela was a heavyweight boxer himself, although he says he enjoyed the science of the sport more than the violence of it.

On Boycotts

By and large, boycotts are recognized and accepted by the people as an effective and powerful weapon of political struggle.

On Change

Belief in the possibility of change and renewal is perhaps one of the defining characteristics of politics and of religions.

On Charity

Cash handouts might sustain you for a few months, at the end of which your problems remain.

On His Childhood

When I was a boy brought up in my village in the Transkei, I listened to the elders of the tribe telling stories about the good old days, before the arrival of the white man.

In his autobiography, Long Walk to Freedom, Mandela writes touchingly about his childhood. His collaborator on the book was Time contributor Richard Stengel; it took eighteen months to write, starting with a manuscript Mandela had begun secretly in his prison cell. They began work daily at 6.45 a.m. – Mandela is an early riser to this day.

I hoped and vowed then that, among the treasures that life might offer me, would be the opportunity to serve my people and make my own humble contribution to the freedom struggle.

The elders would tell us about the liberation and how it was fought by our ancestors in defence of our country, as well as the acts of valour performed by generals and soldiers during those epic days.

On Children

Children are the most vulnerable citizens in any society and the greatest of our treasures.

Nobel Peace Prize ceremony, Norway, 1993.

The children must, at last, play in the open veld, no longer tortured by the pangs of hunger or ravaged by disease or threatened with the scourge of ignorance, molestation and abuse, and no longer required to engage in deeds whose gravity exceeds the demands of their tender years.

The reward of the ending of apartheid will and must be measured by the happiness and welfare of the children.

The children who sleep in the streets, reduced to begging to make a living, are testimony to an unfinished job.

There can be no keener revelation of a society's soul than the way in which it treats its children.

Taken from his summary of the first year of the Nelson Mandela Children's Fund, 1996 (on the Worldwide Web at http://www.web.co.za/mandela/children).

On Christmas

Christmas was the only time we children could have sugar and tea, and we were also given some syrup and bread and a sheep was slaughtered.

In prison they allowed us to buy a packet of sweets or a packet of fruit.

On Circumcision

It is excruciatingly painful but it is supposed to protect you for the rest of your life and to take you from the state of an adolescent to that of a responsible adult who will take tribal tasks upon his shoulders.

The fact that courage is expected of you in the face of the unbearable gives you strength for the rest of your life.

On Clothes

I had a pair of shorts, sandals but no socks, a
sleeveless shirt and no underwear, which is
very humiliating.

Talking to the then editor of French Vogue, December 1993, and
referring to the early days of his imprisonment — a far cry from the
'Madiba style' shirts he has made famous. They are generally made of and
lined with silk — and the pattern is perfectly aligned, making them costly
in terms of fabric.

There isn't a single article I wear that I have
bought — people just generously give me
clothes.

After seven months as President in 1994.

On Colonialism

Through force, fraud and violence, the people
of North, East, West, Central and Southern
Africa were relieved of their political and
economic power and forced to pay allegiance
to foreign monarchs.

The resistance of the black man to white colonial intrusion was crushed by the gun.

Taken from Mandela's letter, smuggled out of Robben Island after the 1976 Soweto uprising, and published internationally by the ANC in 1980.

In all we do, we have to ensure the healing of the wounds inflicted on all our people across the great dividing line imposed on our society by centuries of colonialism and apartheid.

The nineteenth-century colonization of the African continent was in many respects the culmination of the Renaissance-initiated expansion of European dominion over the planet.

On Communication

One of our strongest weapons is dialogue.

On Communism

For many decades communists were the only political group in South Africa who were prepared to treat Africans as human beings and their equals; who were prepared to eat with us; talk with us, live with us and work with us.

Spoken from the dock at the Rivonia Treason Trial, 20 April 1964.

There is so much hypocrisy behind some of this red-baiting that it sickens me, and I feel like saying to the culprits: 'How dare you say to me, a man of seventy-five, that I must denounce my friends, and for whom?'

On Compromise

That is the nature of compromising: you can compromise on fundamental issues.

At one of his first interviews after his release from twenty-seven years' imprisonment, 15 February 1990. He was released on 11 February 1990.

If you are not prepared to compromise, then you must not enter or think about the process of negotiation at all.

Compromise must not undermine your own position.

On Conciliation

No organization whose interests are identical with those of the toiling masses will advocate conciliation to win its demands.

On the South African Constitution

We give life to our nation's prayer for freedom regained and a continent reborn.

On signing the new South African constitution into law at Sharpeville, 10 December 1996.

Let us now, drawing strength from the unity which we have forged, together grasp the opportunities and realize the vision enshrined in this constitution.

Respect for human life, liberty and well-being must be enshrined as rights beyond the power of any force to diminish.

The key to the protection of any minority is to put core civil and political rights beyond the reach of temporary majorities by guaranteeing them as fundamental human rights, enshrined in a democratic constitution.

On Criticism

If the criticism is valid, is must be made.

On His Death

It would be very egotistical of me to say how I would like to be remembered. I'd leave that entirely to South Africans.

There will be life after Mandela.

I would just like a simple stone on which is written, 'Mandela'.

From an interview published in the USA, March 1997.

On Democracy

What is important is not only to attain victory for democracy, it is to retain democracy.

Democracy and human rights are inseparable.

A democratic political order must be based on the majority principle, especially in a country where the vast majority have been systematically denied their rights.

Even tyrants must be allowed to campaign.

Majority rule is not intended to suppress the views, the hopes, the aspirations, of the minority.

On Demonstrations

Mass action is a peaceful form of channelling the anger of the people.

On Determination

As long as you have an iron will you can turn misfortune into advantage.

From a letter to his daughter, Zindzi Mandela, September 1990.

On Discipline

Discipline is the most powerful weapon to get liberation.

On Domesticity

I make my own bed every day. I don't allow
the ladies who look after me to do it. I can
cook a decent meal . . . I can polish a floor.

On Education

Parents have the right to choose the kind of
education that shall be given to their children.

Make every home, every shack or rickety
structure a centre of learning.

On Election Day (27-28 April 1994)

It was as though we were a nation reborn.

We can loudly proclaim from the rooftops –
Free at last! Free at last!

After Martin Luther King, Jnr (the closing words from his 'I Have a Dream' speech, Washington DC, 28 August 1963). Nelson Mandela spoke the words on the first day of the first democratic South African elections, 27 April 1994. He had just voted for the first time in his life – he was seventy-four.

I stand before you humbled by your courage
with a heart full of love for all of you.

On Emigration

To this day we continue to lose some of the
best among ourselves because the lights in the
developed world shine brighter.

On Enemies

If a man fights back he is likely to get more
respect than he would if he capitulated.

At his Bishopscourt, Cape Town, press conference on 15 February 1990, his first after his release from twenty-seven years' jail.

I wanted South Africa to see that I loved even
my enemies while I hated the system that
turned us against one another.

Mandela's presidency has been notable for the efforts he has made towards
reconciliation — including taking tea in the all-white Boer enclave of Oranje with
the widow of the architect of apartheid, Dr Hendrik Verwoerd, and meeting Dr
Percy Yutar, prosecuting attorney at the Rivonia Treason Trial.

Sitting down and denying the enemy the
opportunity to use violence is the best strategy.

On Family

Our families are far larger than those of whites
and it is always a pleasure to be fully accepted
throughout a village, district, or even several
districts, accompanied by your clan, and be a
beloved household member, where you can
call at any time, completely relaxed, sleep at
ease and freely take part in the discussion of
all problems, where you can even be given
livestock and land to build, free of charge.

From an undated letter, written from Robben Island, to his cousin Sisi.

On His Family

I have had to separate myself from my dear
wife and children, from my mother and
sisters, to live as an outlaw in my own land.

To see your family, your children being
persecuted when you are absolutely helpless
in jail, that is one of the most bitter
experiences, most painful experiences, I have
had.

I rued the pain I had often caused my family
through my absence.

I did not in the beginning choose to place my
people above my family, but in attempting to
serve my people, I found I was prevented from
fulfilling my obligations as a son, a brother, a
father and a husband.

*He has said this frequently, and might have added 'and as a grandfather'. In 1997
he had twenty-one grandchildren.*

Our political activities have just destroyed our
family.

*Spoken after two and a half years as President of South Africa and referring,
sadly, to his retirement, which he expects to be spent largely as a global statesman.*

One of my greatest pleasures is to sit down with my children and listen to them, to listen to their hopes and aspirations and helping them to grow.

On Favourite Things

My favourite animal is the impala because it is alert, curious, rapid and able to get out of difficult conditions easily – and with grace.

Taken from French Vogue, December 1993/January 1994. It was a historic issue – edited by Nelson Mandela himself – and now a collector's item.

Koeksisters are my favourite: in 1941 I was paid £2 a month and I reserved 10/- each weekend for koeksisters.

Koeksisters are a sticky Afrikaans sweet: plaited dough, deep fried and dunked in cold syrup.

On Freedom

There is no easy walk to freedom.

He was thirty-five when he made that statement in his famous 'No Easy Walk to Freedom' speech. The words were originally spoken by India's first Prime Minister after independence, Jawaharlal Nehru.

Too many have suffered for the love of freedom.

Still imprisoned, this was from his first speech in almost twenty-five years. It was read in Johannesburg to wildly cheering crowds by his youngest daughter, Zindzi, on 10 February 1985.

Only free men can negotiate.

No power on earth can stop an oppressed people determined to win their freedom.

From 'The Struggle is My Life' press statement, 26 June 1961.

There is no such thing as part freedom.

Freedom cannot be given in doses; one is either free or not free – not half free.

Only through hardship, sacrifice and militant action can freedom be won.

No South African should rest and wallow in the joy of freedom.

To men, freedom in their own land is the pinnacle of their ambitions, from which nothing can turn men of conviction aside.

We do not want freedom without bread, nor do we want bread without freedom.

Freedom is not only the opportunity to vote, but the gate to the awareness of many problems: hunger, poverty, illness, non-advancement.

To overthrow oppression is the highest aspiration of every free man.

From Mandela's 'Black Man in a White Court' statement at his trial held in the Old Synagogue, Pretoria, from 15 October 1962 to 7 November 1962.

A man who takes away another man's freedom is a prisoner of hatred.

After twenty-seven years' imprisonment, Nelson Mandela walked to freedom through the gates of Victor Verster Prison, Paarl, at 4.16 p.m. on 11 February 1990.

Freedom cannot be achieved unless women have been emancipated from all forms of oppression.

To be free is not merely to cast off one's chains, but to live in a way that respects and enhances the lives of others.

On the Freedom Charter (1955)

The Freedom Charter is a political programme born of our struggle and rooted in South African realities.

It has received international acclaim as an outstanding human rights document.

The Charter is more than a mere list of demands for democratic reforms.

On Friendship

Friendship and support from friends is something which is a source of tremendous inspiration always and to everyone.

On Government

When a government seeks to suppress a peaceful demonstration of an unarmed people by mobilizing the entire reserves of the state, military and police, it concedes powerful mass support for such a demonstration.

Said in 1961 when he was in hiding and was referred to as the Black Pimpernel in the nation's press. A monument has now been erected near the spot where he was finally arrested on the night of 5 July 1962 outside the KwaZulu/Natal town of Howick.

That the will of the people is the basis of the authority of government is a principle universally acknowledged as sacred throughout the civilized world, and constitutes the basic foundations of freedom and justice.

Even when a democratic government is installed, no minority group should be disadvantaged.

There is always a danger that when there is no opposition, the governing party can become too arrogant – too confident of itself.

On Government Corruption

Corruption in government – that is a plague that must be erased from every regime in every place in the world.

On Harlem, New York

Harlem symbolizes the strength and beauty in resistance and you have taught us that out of resistance to injustice comes renaissance, renewal and rebirth.

On Health

The wounds that cannot be seen are more painful than those that can be treated by a doctor.

On Heroes

No single individual can assume the role of hero or Messiah.

There are men and women chosen to bring happiness into the hearts of people – those are the real heroes.

On His Heroes

Muhammed Ali was an inspiration to me even in prison because I thought of his courage and commitment. He used mind and body in unison and achieved success.

Kobie Coetsee – I have immense respect for that man because when no member of the National Party wanted to hear about the ANC, he was working systematically with me. He is one of my heroes.

Kobie Coetsee was Minister of Justice under P.W. Botha.

On Himself

I have always regarded myself, in the first place, as an African patriot.

From the dock at the Rivonia Treason Trial, 20 April 1964. It took him two weeks, working in his cell at night, to write the speech.

I am a product of the mire that our society was.

I don't think there is much history can say about me.

I wanted to be able to stand and fight with my people and to share the hazards of war with them.

From the Rivonia Treason Trial, 20 April 1964.

I was made, by the law, a criminal, not because of what I had done, but because of what I stood for, because of what I thought, because of my conscience.

Spoken at the Old Synagogue Trial, Pretoria, 7 November 1962.

I am not a prophet and I am not in a position to say what we hope and desire in our lifetime.

I saw my mission as one of preaching reconciliation, of binding the wounds of the country, of engendering trust and confidence.

I felt fear more times than I can remember, but I hid it behind a mask of boldness.

I have always been a member of the African National Congress and I will remain a member of the African National Congress until the day I die.

I'm an ordinary person, I have made serious mistakes, I have serious weaknesses.

I will pass through this world but once, and I do not want to divert my attention from my task, which is to unite the nation.

Spoken in February 1996 when he was seventy-seven.

Sometimes I feel like one who is on the sidelines, who has missed life itself.

Rather than being an asset, I'm more of a decoration.

Referring to himself as President of South Africa.

People expect me to do more than is humanly possible.

I carry with me the frailties of my age and the fetters of prejudice that are a privilege of my years.

He said this in 1997 to the International Olympic Committee, Lausanne, in a bid to persuade them to bring the Olympics to Cape Town in 2004.

I seem to arrive more firmly at the conclusion that my own life struggle has had meaning only because, dimly and perhaps incoherently, it has sought to achieve the supreme objective of ensuring that each, without regard to race, colour, gender or social status, could have the possibility to reach for the skies.

On History

History punishes those who resort to force
and fraud to suppress the claims and
legitimate aspirations of the majority of the
country's citizens.

History shows that penalties do not deter men
when their conscience is aroused.

Ordinary South Africans are determined that
the past be known, the better to ensure that it
is not repeated.

Blaming things on the past does not make
them better.

The past is a rich resource on which we can
draw in order to make decisions for the
future.

The purpose of studying history is not to
deride human action, nor to weep over it or
to hate it, but to understand it — and then to
learn from it as we contemplate our future.

On Home

I long to see the little stones on which I played
as a child, the little rivers, where I swam.

Spoken with longing just after his release in 1990. When Nelson Mandela built
his own house in Qunu, Transkei, where he was brought up, he built the house
identically to the one he had lived in at Victor Verster Prison, Paarl. To this day, he
says he was happiest between 1988 and 1990.

Everybody comes back to where they were
born.

He was spending Christmas 1996 at Qunu. But for the years of his
imprisonment, it was the modest Sowetan house he shared with Winnie – No.
8115, Orlando West – which he dreamt about. In May 1997, together with his
partner Graça Machel, he bought a new home in Houghton, Johannesburg,
specifically to make space for his twenty-one grandchildren, some of whom live
with him for extended periods.

On Homosexuality

There was a time when I reacted with
revulsion against the whole system of being
gay.

I was ashamed of my initial views, coming from a society which did not know this type of thing.

I understand their position, and I think they are entitled to carry on with what pleases them.

On His Hopes

Should (we not) begin to define the national interest to include the genuine happiness of others, however distant in time and space their domicile might be?

Many of us will have to pass through the valley of the shadow of death again and again before we reach the mountain tops of our desires.

On Housing

A man is not a man until he has a house of his own.

The families who live in shacks with no running water, sanitation and electricity are a reminder that the past continues to haunt the present.

On Humanity

It is what we make out of what we have, not what we are given, that separates one person from another.

It is a fact of the human condition that each shall, like a meteor – a mere brief passing moment in time and space – flit across the human stage and pass out of existence.

From his address to the Joint Session of the Houses of Congress of the USA, 26 June 1990, where he was rapturously received only months after his release.

To deny any person their human rights is to challenge their very humanity.

We fought injustice to preserve our own humanity.

Referring to the Robben Island years.

Deep down in every human heart, there is mercy and generosity.

Human beings have multiple lives and identities within and across racial and ethnic lines.

Let the strivings of us all prove Martin Luther King, Jnr to have been correct when he said that humanity can no longer be tragically bound to the starless midnight of racism and war.

What challenges us is to ensure that none should enjoy lesser rights; and none tormented because they are born different, hold contrary political views, or pray to God in a different manner.

We have fights as human beings, but you should never forget that we are the creation of one Lord.

The world is one stage and the actions of all inhabitants part of the same drama.

None of us can be described as having virtues or qualities that raise him or her above others.

After climbing a great hill, one finds that there are many more hills to climb.

The universe we inhabit as human beings is becoming a common home that shows growing disrespect for the rigidities imposed on humanity by national boundaries.

On Imperialism

Imperialism means the denial of political and economic rights and the perpetual subjugation of the people by a foreign power.

Imperialism has been weighed and found wanting.

On Inauguration Day, 10 May 1994

One of the outstanding human victories of the century.

The time for the healing of the wounds has come. The moment to bridge the chasms that divide us has come. The time to build is upon us.

Taken from his speech. His inauguration as President of South Africa was held at the Union Buildings in Pretoria, a day no South African who watched it will ever forget.

On Islam

Islam has enriched and become part of Africa; in turn, Islam was transformed and Africa became part of it.

On Jellybeans

What are jellybeans? Are they something that is eaten?

In a Radio Good Hope interview, May 1996.

On Leadership

It is a mistake to think that a single individual can unite the country.

When leaders have the honesty to criticize their own mistakes and their own organization, then they can criticize others.

Many in positions of power and privilege pursue cold-hearted philosophies which terrifyingly proclaim: I am not your brother's keeper!

A leadership commits a crime against its own people if it hesitates to sharpen its political weapons which have become less effective.

It is no use for a leader to surround himself with yes-men.

A leader who relies on authority to solve problems is bound to come to grief.

We have the high salaries and we are living in luxury: that destroys our capacity to speak in a forthright manner and tell people to tighten their belts.

From a September 1994 interview – some four months after Mandela was inaugurated as President of South Africa.

It is important to surround yourself with strong and independent personalities, who will tell you when you are getting old.

Nelson Mandela said this in 1996 when there was speculation about his health and queries were being raised in South Africa as to whether he would be able to complete his term of office.

On Liberation

The people are their own liberators.

On Literature

We could not have made an acquaintance through literature with human giants such as George Washington, Abraham Lincoln and Thomas Jefferson and not been moved to act as they were moved to act.

On Love

The world is truly round and seems to start and end with those we love.

From a letter to Winnie, 1 July 1979.

I am not nervous of love for love is very inspiring.

Spoken on his state visit to the UK, July 1996. Only a few people at that time knew of his love for Graça Machel, widow of Samora Machel, first President of Mozambique.

To be in love is an experience that every man must go through.

One should be so grateful at being involved in such an experience.

It is such a wonderful period for me.

Spoken in April 1997, and referring to his relationship with Graça Machel.

On Marriage

The whole purpose of a husband and wife is
that when hard times knock at the door you
should be able to embrace each other.

According to our custom, you marry the
village and not the human being.

A man and wife usually discuss their most
intimate problems in the bedroom.

Spoken in March 1996, in public, at his divorce hearing from his second
wife, Winnie.

Ladies don't want to be marrying an old man
like me.

On being asked whether he would marry Graça Machel (1996).

On Men

Men must follow the dictates of their
conscience irrespective of the consequences
which might overtake them for it.

On Misfortunes

There are few misfortunes in this world that you cannot turn into a personal triumph if you have the iron will and the necessary skill.

On Morality

A movement without a vision is a movement without moral foundation.

On the National Party

Where were they when our people died at the hands of the police?

We are hopeful that, in their role, they will add another brick into the edifice of our young democracy.

For people that had to invoke the name of God as they made our people suffer? For people who warped the concept of Christianity to cloak the abomination of apartheid in it?

Incredulously referring to the National Party, the bulwark of apartheid until 1994, versus the South African Communist Party.

On Negotiation

Concessions are inherent in negotiations.

It is difficult to negotiate with those who do not share the same frame of reference.

When you negotiate you have to accept the integrity of another man.

When you negotiate you must be prepared to compromise.

On the New World Order

Is the time not upon us when we should cease
to treat tyranny, instability and poverty
anywhere on our globe as being peripheral to
our interests and to our future?

Can we say with confidence that it is within
our reach to declare that never again shall
continents, countries or communities be
reduced to the smoking battlefields of
contending forces of nationality, religion, race
or language?

From his lecture at the Oxford Centre for Islamic Studies, July 1997.

As the world frees itself from the dominance
of bi-polar power the stark division of the
world's people into rich and poor comes all
the more clearly into view.

Intervention only works when the people
concerned seem to be keen for peace.

If I have any moral authority – and I say if –
moral authority doesn't solve world problems.

The reality can no longer be ignored that we live in an interdependent world which is bound together to a common destiny.

On the Nobel Peace Prize

Let it never be said by future generations that indifference, cynicism or selfishness made us fail to live up to the ideals of humanism which the Nobel Peace Prize encapsulates.

Nobel Peace Prize ceremony, Norway, 10 December 1993. He received the award jointly with F.W. de Klerk, at that time still State President of South Africa. The Nobel Peace Prize had a special meaning to him, because his award was preceded by another two South Africans: Chief Albert Luthuli, former president of the ANC, was a Nobel Peace Prize winner, as was Archbishop Desmond Tutu.

On Oppression

To overthrow oppression has been sanctioned
by humanity and is the highest aspiration of
every free man.

From his famous 'No Easy Walk To Freedom' speech, 1953.

On Peace

Peace and democracy go hand in hand.

It is not easy to talk about peace to people
who are mourning every day.

To some, talking about peace is a sign of
cowardice – but in fact it is a sign of strength.

Everyone must fight for peace.

I will go down on my knees to beg those who want to drag our country into bloodshed and persuade them not to do so.

Our most effective weapon is peace and love for our fellow man.

On People

I love you. You are my own flesh and blood. Your are my brothers, sisters, children and grandchildren.

Speaking to the people of South Africa.

I surely wish the pockets of my shirt were big enough to fit all of you in.

To his compatriots in the Transkei.

In life, every man has twin obligations — obligations to his family, to his parents, to his wife and children; and he has an obligation to his people, his community and his country.

Which man of honour will desert a lifelong friend at the insistence of a common opponent and still retain a measure of credibility with his people?

From an open letter to P.W. Botha, State President of South Africa, who had offered him a conditional freedom. Mandela's youngest daughter, Zindzi, read it to a rapt crowd at the Jabulani Stadium, Soweto, on 10 February 1985.

Language, culture and religion are important indicators of identity.

Justice and liberty must be our tool, prosperity and happiness our weapon.

On Personalities

Steve Biko, murdered black consciousness activist

There can be no doubt that he was one of the most talented and colourful freedom fighters South Africa has produced.

P.W. Botha, Former State President

The thing that impressed me was that he poured the tea.

After their first meeting, 4 July 1989. Mandela was still behind bars in Cape Town's Pollsmoor Prison. So unused was he to shoes with laces, that one of his captors had to tie them for him.

Mangosuthu Buthelezi, IFP President, Minister of Home Affairs

When we are together, he is very, very courteous. But when he is away from you, he behaves totally differently, because he does not know if he is still your friend or not.

The problem is when he leaves the cabinet and appears on public platforms. Then he behaves like any other politician.

Bill Clinton, US President

There is a vow of goodwill between us.

F.W. de Klerk, Former State President

He had the courage to admit that a terrible wrong had been done to our country and people through the imposition of the system of apartheid.

If there is anything that has cooled relations between me and Mr de Klerk, it is his paralysis as far as violence is concerned.

This was said in September 1992, with reference to the Boipatong massacre and the increasingly inexplicable 'third force' violence in South Africa; in view of Mr de Klerk's much criticized submissions to the Truth and Reconciliation Commission, it was a prophetic remark.

His tactic is to praise the President and then attack and undermine the ANC.

In a September 1994 interview with The New York Times.

Diana, Princess of Wales

I found her very graceful, highly intelligent, and committed to worthy causes and I was tremendously impressed by her warmth.

Queen Elizabeth II

The Queen is a very gracious lady and I'm
sure she'll put a country boy at ease.

On the eve of his historic — and jubilant — state visit to Britain, July 1996.

Muammar Gaddafi, President of Libya

He helped us at a time when we were all
alone, when those who are now saying we
should not come here were helping our
enemies.

*Said at the start of his controversial October 1997 visit to Libya in the face
of UN and US disapproval.*

Mahatma Gandhi

It would not be right to compare me to
Gandhi. None of us could equal his dedication
or his humility.

He showed us that it was necessary to brave
imprisonment if truth and justice were to
triumph over evil.

We must never lose sight of the fact that the Gandhian philosophy may be a key to human survival in the twenty-first century.

Jose Xana Gusmão, imprisoned East Timorese leader

It was regrettable that a man of his talents should languish in jail.

There are poignant similarities between Gusmão's plight and that of Mandela. Gusmão has been sentenced to prison for twenty years for opposing the Indonesian invasion of his country; his latter-day champion is Nelson Mandela.

Chris Hani, assassinated leader of the ANC Youth League

A white man, full of prejudice and hate, came to our country and committed a deed so foul that our whole nation now teeters on the brink of disaster. A white woman, of Afrikaner origin, risked her life so that we may know, and bring to justice, this assassin.

Speech to all South Africans, calming the angry youth after Hani's assassination at the hands of a white man, 10 April 1992.

Bishop Trevor Huddleston

His sacrifices for our freedom told us that the true relationship between our people was not one between poor citizens on the one hand and good patricians on the other, but one underwritten by our common humanity and our human capacity to touch one another's hearts across the oceans.

Martin Luther King, Jnr

He grappled with and died in the effort to make a contribution to the just solution of the same great issues of the day which we have had to face as South Africans.

From his Nobel Peace Prize address, 10 December 1993.

Thabo Mbeki, Deputy President of South Africa

He is polite but he is not a yes-man. He will always stand his ground.

Cyril Ramaphosa, trade unionist, politician, negotiator and businessman

He is a son to me.

A young man of considerable ability destined to occupy a very important position in our political life.

Jonas Savimbi, Angolan rebel leader

I don't think he wants to play second fiddle.

President Suharto, Indonesian leader

Suharto is an able, patient and suave leader but he can become firm when one raises issues about which he has strong feelings.

Oliver Tambo, Former President of the ANC

He is my greatest friend and comrade for fifty years.

Oliver Tambo was Nelson Mandela's lifelong friend. They were in law practice together. Later President of the ANC, Tambo lived most of his life in exile. He returned to South Africa, but died shortly afterwards, not living long enough to see his dream of a democratic South Africa realized.

Archbishop Desmond Tutu, Nobel Laureate

He's a terrific fellow.

He has been a blessing and inspiration to countless people through his ministry; his acts of compassion; his prophetic witness; and his political engagement.

Said at a thanksgiving service for the ministry of Archbishop Tutu, June 1996.

On Photography

Good use of photography will give even poverty with all its rags, filth and vermin a measure of divineness rarely noticeable in real life.

From a letter to Zindzi, 6 August 1979.

On Politics

Political division, based on colour, is entirely artificial and, when it disappears, so will the domination of one colour group by another.

From the dock at the Rivonia Treason Trial, 20 April 1964.

A political movement must keep in touch with reality and the prevailing conditions.

Political power should be the basis for the economic empowerment of people.

We should not allow South African politics to be relegated to trivialities chosen precisely because they salve the consciences of the rich and powerful, and conceal the plight of the poor and powerless.

If you are a politician you must be prepared to suffer for your principles.

On Poverty

It should never be that the anger of the poor should be the finger of accusation pointed at all of us because we failed to respond to the cries of the people for food, for shelter, for the dignity of the individual.

On Praise

The exaltation of the President, and denigration of other ANC leaders, constitutes praise which I do not accept.

On Being President (of South Africa)

This has placed a great responsibility on my shoulders.

We enter into a covenant that we shall build a society in which all South Africans, both black and white, will be able to walk tall, without any fear in their hearts, assured of their inalienable right to human dignity – a rainbow nation at peace with itself and the world.

From his Inauguration speech, 10 May 1994.

At the end of my term I'll be eighty-one. I don't think it's wise that a robust country like South Africa should be led by a septuagenarian.

Spoken in 1996 when there were rumours about his health. A septuagenarian when he made the comment, he would, of course, be an octogenarian at the end of his term of office.

It is a way of life in which it's hard to dedicate time to the things that are really close to your heart.

To be the father of a nation is a great honour, but to be the father of a family is a greater joy.

My present life, even if it's not the easiest way of life, is very rewarding.

Spoken in mid 1997, one of his busiest years.

On the Press

A critical, independent and investigative press is the lifeblood of any democracy.

It was the press who never forgot us.

Spoken just after his release, February 1990.

A press conference is not a place to discuss rumours.

It is only a free press that can temper the appetite of any government to amass power at the expense to the citizen.

The press is one of the pillars of democracy.

On Prison

Nothing is more dehumanizing than isolation from human companionship.

Nelson Mandela saw Robben Island for the first time from Table Mountain, Cape Town, in 1947. Less than twenty years later he was incarcerated there.

The long, lonely wasted years.

He was prisoner 466/64.

There I had time to just sit for hours and think.

On Punctuality

A lack of punctuality is something which shows lack of respect for the organization and those appointed into positions, and a lack of self-respect.

On Racism

Death to racism.

I detest racialism, because I regard it as a barbaric thing, whether it comes from a black man or a white man.

Racism pollutes the atmosphere of human relations and poisons the minds of the backward, the bigoted and the prejudiced.

Our struggle is the struggle to erase the colour line that all too often determines who is rich and who is poor.

As we enter the last decade of the twentieth century, it is intolerable and unacceptable that the cancer of racism is still eating away at the fabric of societies in different parts of our planet.

We must ensure that colour, race and gender become only a God-given gift to each one of us and not an indelible mark or attribute that accords a special status to any.

We shall never again allow our country to play host to racism. Nor shall our voices be stilted if we see that another, elsewhere in the world, is victim to racial tyranny.

Racism must be consciously combated and not discreetly tolerated.

The very fact that racism degrades both the perpetrator and the victim commands that, if we are true to our commitment to protect human dignity, we fight on until victory is achieved.

All of us know how stubbornly racism can cling to the mind and how deeply it can infect the human soul.

It will perhaps come to be that we who have harboured in our country the worst example of racism since the defeat of Nazism, will make a contribution to human civilization by ordering our affairs in such a manner that we strike an effective and lasting blow against racism everywhere.

I hate the practice of race discrimination, and in my hatred I am sustained by the fact that the overwhelming majority of mankind hate it equally.

On Reconciliation

The mission of reconciliation is underpinned by what I have dedicated my life to: uplifting the most downtrodden sections of our population and all round transformation of society.

We need to reconcile our differences through reason, debate and compromise.

Without reconciliation, we will not be able to give our people a better life.

Reconstruction goes hand in hand with reconciliation.

On His Release

I would be merely rationalizing if I told you that I am able to describe my own feelings. It was breathtaking, that is all I can say.

Along the route (from Paarl to Cape Town) I was surprised to see the number of whites who seemed to identify themselves with what is happening to the country today amongst blacks.

I was completely overwhelmed by the enthusiasm.

On Religion

The simple lesson of religions, of all philosophies and of life itself is that, although evil may be on the rampage temporarily, the good must win the laurels in the end.

From a letter to his friend Fatima Meer, 1 January 1976. Less than six months later, the Soweto uprising broke out, signalling the eventual end of apartheid.

Religion runs in our veins.

Referring to South Africans.

The strength of inter-religious solidarity in action against apartheid, rather than mere harmony or coexistence, was critical in bringing that evil system to an end.

(African traditional religion) is no longer seen as despised superstition which had to be superseded by superior forms of belief; today its enrichment of humanity's spiritual heritage is acknowledged.

On Retirement

I must step down while there are one or two people who admire me.

November 1996, when he was seventy-eight.

I intend to do a bit of farming when I step down. I will be without a job and I don't want to find myself standing at the side of the road with a placard saying: unemployed.

There is no reason whatsoever for anyone to think there will be dislocation in South Africa

as a result of the stepping down of an
individual.

On Revenge

You can't build a united nation on the basis of
revenge.

*In an interview with The New York Times in March 1997; he was referring
to the Truth and Reconciliation Commission.*

On the South African Right Wing

There are still powerful elements among
whites who are not reconciled with the
present transformation and who want to use
every excuse to drown the country in
bloodshed.

There are still some within our country who
wrongly believe they can make a contribution
to the cause of justice and peace by clinging to
the shibboleths that have been proved to spell
nothing but disaster.

On the Rugby World Cup, South Africa, 1995

When I left the stadium my nerves were completely shattered.

I'm still recovering.

When it was 12–12 I almost collapsed. I was absolutely tense.

Our whole nation stood behind a sport which was once a symbol of apartheid.

None more so than Nelson Mandela himself. He appeared at the final wearing captain François Pienaar's No. 6 shirt – and brought the entire country along with him, surely one of the most successful efforts at reconciliation in South Africa.

On Rwanda

Rwanda stands out as a stern and severe rebuke to all of us.

The louder and more piercing the cries of despair – even when that despair results in half a million dead in Rwanda – the more these cries seem to encourage an instinctive reaction to raise our hands so as to close our eyes and ears.

None of us can insulate ourselves from so catastrophic a scale of human suffering.

On Sabotage

I planned it as a result of a calm and sober assessment of the situation, after many years of oppression and tyranny of my people by the whites.

From the Rivonia Treason Trial, 20 April 1964 – the trial which sent him to prison for twenty-seven years.

On Self-respect

If you are in harmony with yourself, you may
meet a lion without fear, because he respects
anyone with self-confidence.

On Soccer

Soccer is one of the sporting disciplines in
which Africa is rising to demonstrate her
excellence, for too long latent in her womb.

On Society

The great lesson of our time is that no regime
can survive if it acts above the heads of the
ordinary citizens of the country.

On South Africa

We are marching to a new future based on a sound basis of respect.

We live with the hope that as she battles to remake herself, South Africa will be like a microcosm of the new world that is striving to be born.

From his Nobel Peace Prize address, 10 December 1993.

Each time one of us touches the soil of this land, we feel a sense of personal renewal.

Never and never again shall it be that this beautiful land will again experience the oppression of one by another and suffer the indignity of being the skunk of the world.

From his moving Inauguration speech, 10 May 1994.

No society emerging out of the grand disaster of the apartheid system could avoid carrying the blemishes of its past.

If we are able today to speak proudly of a 'rainbow nation', it is in part because the world set us a moral example which we dared to follow.

Had the new South Africa emerged out of nothing, it would not exist.

The first founding stone of our new country is national reconciliation and national unity. The fact that it has settled in its mortar needs no advertising.

We do face major challenges, but none are as daunting as those we have already surmounted.

On receiving the Freedom of the City of London, July 1996.

Never and never again shall the laws of our land rend our people apart or legalize their oppression and repression.

We must work for the day when we, as South Africans, see one another and interact with one another as equal human beings and as part of one nation united, rather than torn asunder, by its diversity.

On South Africans

We are all one nation in one country.

Each one of us is as intimately attached to the soil of this beautiful country as are the famous jacaranda trees of Pretoria and the mimosa trees of the bushveld.

From his Inauguration speech, 10 May 1994.

My country is rich in the minerals and gems that lie beneath its soil, but I have always known that its greatest wealth is its people, finer and truer than the purest diamonds.

It is our privilege as South Africans to be living at a time when our nation is emerging from the darkest night into the bright dawn of freedom and democracy.

Pride in our country is a common bond between us all. It is the essence of our new patriotism.

The onus is on us, through hard work, honesty and integrity, to reach for the stars.

With all our colours and races combined in one nation, we are an African people.

On Sport

Sport can reach out to people in a way which politicians can't.

On The Struggle

The Struggle is my life.

From his famous press statement of 26 June 1961, whilst living underground as the Black Pimpernel.

Struggle that does not strengthen organization can lead to a blind alley.

Struggle without discipline can lead to anarchy.

Struggle without unity enables the other side to pick us off one by one.

No organization whose interests are identical with those of the toiling masses will advocate conciliation to win its demands.

From Liberation, June 1953.

On Survival

For me, survival is the ability to cope with difficulties, with circumstances, and to overcome them.

On Sweden

We have become political neighbours who willingly share whatever little bread and salt we may have.

On Talk

Rhetoric is not important. Actions are.

On Thoughts

We must think through our heads, not
through our blood.

On Tolerance

You should be tolerant to those who have
views that are different to yours, because you
will win by the correctness of the position that
you take.

On Truth

No matter how hard its adversary — falsehood
— may try to overwhelm it, truth refuses to
yield.

On the Truth and Reconciliation Commission

Above all the healing process involves the nation, because it is the nation itself that needs to redeem and reconstruct itself.

The Truth and Reconciliation Commission started its work in February 1996. It has heard of atrocities from the right and left, has heard testimony from murderers and torturers — and also from victims and the families of dead victims. It is intended to be an instrument of reconciliation and not of revenge.

All South Africans face the challenge of coming to terms with the past in ways which will enable us to face the future as a united nation at peace with itself.

Some criticize us when we say that whilst we can forgive, we can never forget.

Ordinary South Africans are determined that the past be known, the better to ensure that it is not repeated.

On Ubuntu

The spirit of Ubuntu – that profound African sense that we are human only through the humanity of other human beings – is not a parochial phenomenon, but has added globally to our common search for a better world.

There are numerous definitions of ubuntu – kindness towards human beings is perhaps too mild; as Mandela says, it is to do with one's humanity being enriched by another's.

On the United Kingdom

Your right to determine your own destiny was used to deny us to determine our own.

From his speech to the House of Commons, 5 May 1993.

This country has produced men and women whose names are well known in South Africa, because they, together with thousands of others of your citizens, stood up to oppose this evil system and helped to bring us to where we are today.

We return to this honoured place with neither pikes nor a desire for revenge nor even a plea to your distinguished selves to assuage our hunger for bread. We come to you as friends.

From his historic speech to both Houses of Parliament, London, 11 July 1996.

In a sense, I leave a part of my being here.

Receiving the Freedom of the City of London, July 1996.

The UK, as one of the bastions of democracy, has an obligation to ensure that we have all the material needs to entrench democracy in our country.

I love every one of you. You must understand that the people of South Africa are very grateful to you.

Addressing a crowd of 10 000 from the balcony of South Africa House, Trafalgar Square, London, July 1996.

I regard the British parliament as the most democratic institution in the world, and the independence and impartiality of its judiciary never fail to arouse my admiration.

From the Rivonia Treason Trial, 20 April 1964.

On the USA

We are linked by nature, but proud of each other by choice.

The stand you took established the understanding among the millions of our people that here we have friends, here we have fighters against racism who feel hurt because we are hurt, who seek our success because they too seek the victory of democracy over tyranny.

Address to the Joint Session of the Houses of Congress of the USA, September 1994.

Let us keep our arms locked together so that we form a solid phalanx against racism.

You have felt and recognized that our success advances the very principles on which this country is founded.

How can they have the arrogance to dictate to us where we should go or who our friends should be?

A heated comment made at a dinner in Johannesburg in October 1997 on the eve of his controversial visit to Libya. The USA had expressed its disapproval.

On Violence

Government violence can do only one thing,
and that is to breed counter-violence.

Take your guns, your knives and your pangas,
and throw them into the sea.

His first speech in the troubled province of KwaZulu/Natal after his release from prison, 25 February 1990.

People who kill children are no better than
animals.

Use violence only in self-defence.

In the end, the cries of the infant who dies
because of hunger or because a machete has
slit open its stomach, will penetrate the noises
of the modern city and its sealed windows to
say: am I not human too!

From his historic speech to both Houses of Parliament, London, 11 July 1996.

On Virtue

Virtue and generosity will be rewarded in ways that one cannot know.

On The Vote

On numerous occasions it has been proven in history that people can enjoy the vote even if they have no education.

A vote without food, shelter and health care would be to create the appearance of equality while actual inequality is entrenched.

On White South Africans

The majority of white men regard it as the destiny of the white race to dominate the man of colour.

From the ANC Youth League Manifesto of 1944, largely written by him.

White supremacy implies black inferiority.

From the dock at the Rivonia Treason Trial, 20 April 1964.

Just as many whites have killed just as many blacks.

Asked about deaths of white civilians in ANC attacks, 1990.

Whites fear the reality of democracy.

As long as whites think in terms of group rights they are talking the language of apartheid.

Spoken before the April 1994 elections.

Whites are fellow South Africans and we want them to feel safe, and we appreciate the contribution they have made towards the development of this country.

They have had education, they have got the knowledge, skills and expertise. We want that knowledge and expertise now that we are building our country.

The whites still think as if there were no blacks, or coloureds or Indians.

Said on his wildly successful state visit to the United Kingdom, July 1996.

On Winnie

I had hoped to build you a refuge, no matter how small, so that we would have a place for rest and sustenance before the arrival of the sad, dry days.

From a letter to Winnie from Robben Island, 26 June 1977. They were married 15 June 1958.

Had it not been for your visits, wonderful letters and your love, I would have fallen apart many years ago.

From a letter to Winnie, 6 May 1979.

I have often wondered whether any kind of commitment can ever be sufficient excuse for abandoning a young and inexperienced woman in a pitiless desert.

Letter to Winnie after her 1986 'boxes of matches' speech.

I am convinced that your pain and suffering was far greater than my own.

From his first speech as a free man, Cape Town, 11 February 1990.

I embrace her with all the love and affection I have nursed for her inside and outside prison from the moment I first met her.

Announcing his separation from Winnie, 13 April 1992.

My love for her remains undiminished.

Part of his poignant separation announcement.

I was the loneliest man during the period I stayed with her.

During his divorce trial, March 1996.

On Women

The beauty of a woman lies as much in her face as in her body.

From a letter to his daughter Zindzi, 5 March 1978.

If a pretty woman walks by, I don't want to be out of the running.

An aside to correspondent Patti Waldmeir at a dinner.

On Work

Job, jobs and jobs are the dividing line in many families between a decent life and a wretched existence.

Workers need a living wage – and the right to join unions of their own choice and to participate in determining policies that affect their lives.

On Writing

Writing is a prestigious profession which puts one right into the centre of the world and, to remain on top, one has to work really hard, the aim being a good and original theme, simplicity in expression and the use of the irreplaceable word.

From a letter to his daughter Zindzi, 4 September 1977.

On Youth

I admire young people who are concerned
with the affairs of their community and nation
perhaps because I also became involved in
struggle whilst I was still at school.

Young people are capable, when aroused, of
bringing down the towers of oppression and
raising the banners of freedom.

I appeal to the youth and all those on the
ground: start talking to each other across
divisions of race and political organizations.

I pay tribute to the endless heroism of youth.

Whenever I am with energetic young people,
I feel like a recharged battery.

On Zulus

No people can boast more proudly of having ploughed a significant field in the Struggle.

Zulus have fought a long struggle against oppression.

The Battle of Isandlwana in 1879 has been an inspiration for those of us engaged in the struggle for justice and freedom in South Africa.

The battle took place on 22 January 1879; some 20 000 Zulu warriors mowed down the invading British Army under Lord Chelmsford camped beneath the mountain of Isandlwana; part of the Zulu army — some 5 000 men — then went on to attack Rorke's Drift on the night of Isandlwana. Rorke's Drift withstood the onslaught, earning for its defenders eleven Victoria Crosses.

When my sentence has been completed I will still be moved, as men are always moved, by their consciences; I will still be moved by my dislike of the race discrimination against my people when I come out from serving my sentence, to take up again, as best I can, the struggle for the removal of those injustices until they are finally abolished once and for all.

Spoken in court, on 7 November 1962, at the end of the Old Synagogue Trial, when he was convicted and sentenced to three years' imprisonment on charges of incitement and two years' imprisonment for leaving South Africa without valid travel documents.

Sources

Mary Benson, *Nelson Mandela: The Man and the Movement* (Penguin, Harmondsworth, 1994)

H.H.W. de Villiers, *Rivonia — Operation Mayibuye: A Review of the Rivonia Trial* (Afrikaanse Pers-Boekhandel, Johannesburg, 1964)

The Historic Speech of Nelson Rolihlahla Mandela at the Rivonia Trial (Learn & Teach Publications, Johannesburg, 1964)

Nelson Mandela, *The Struggle is My Life* (Pathfinder, New York, 1991)

Fatima Meer, *Higher Than Hope* (Penguin, Harmondsworth, 1990)

Patti Waldmeir, *Anatomy of a Miracle* (Viking, London, 1997)

ANC Youth League Manifesto, 1944; AP; *The Argus*; *Business Day*; *Cape Times*; *The Citizen*; *Daily Telegraph*; *Financial Times*; *Liberation*; *Mail & Guardian*; *Natal Witness*; *The New York Times*; *RSA Review 1995*; SAPA; *Saturday Star*; *Sowetan*; *The Star*; *The Sunday Independent*; *Sunday Telegraph*; *Sunday Times*; *Time*; *Vogue* (French edition), Dec 1993/Jan 1994

Radio Good Hope; Radio 702; M-Net; No

Easy Walk to Freedom speech, 21 September
1953; Shifting Sands of Illusion article,
Liberation, June 1953; Freedom in Our Lifetime
article, *Liberation*, June 1956; A New Menace
in Africa article, *Liberation*, March 1958;
Verwoerd's Tribalism speech, May 1959; The
Struggle is My Life press statement, 26 June
1961; Letter to the Prime Minister, Dr H.F.
Verwoerd, 26 June 1961; Address to the
Conference of the Pan-African Freedom
Movement of East and South Africa, Addis
Ababa, January 1962; Black Man in a White
Court Trial speech, the Old Synagogue,
Pretoria, 7 November 1962; Rivonia Treason
Trial speech, 20 April 1964; letter to his
daughter Zindzi, 4 September 1977;
Mandela's Call to the Youth of South Africa
smuggled speech, 1980; Whilst Still in Prison,
his first speech in almost twenty-five years,
defiantly read by his daughter Zindzi, 10
February 1985; release from Victor Verster
Prison speech, Cape Town, 11 February 1990;
Bishopscourt press conference, 12 February
1990; FNB Stadium (Soccer City) speech,
Johannesburg, 13 February 1990;
Bloemfontein speech, 25 February 1990;
Durban Rally speech, 25 February 1990;
address to the Swedish parliament, 13 March

1990; Harlem speech, New York City, 21 June 1990; address to the Joint Session of the Houses of Congress of the USA, 26 June 1990; announcement of his separation from Winnie, 13 April 1992; Gandhi Hall, Lenasia, speech, 27 September 1992; speech to the House of Commons, London, 5 May 1993; acceptance address at the Clark University Investiture, Atlanta, 10 July 1993; Nobel Peace Prize award ceremony speech, Oslo, 10 December 1993; ANC election victory speech, 2 May 1994; Inauguration speech, 10 May 1994; address to the forty-ninth session of the General Assembly, United Nations, New York City, 3 October 1994; Business Leaders speech, New Delhi, 26 January 1995; African Cup of Nations Tournament speech, 13 January 1996; Interfaith Commissioning Service for the Truth and Reconciliation Commission speech, 13 February 1996; University of Potchefstroom speech, 19 February 1996; Opening of Parliament speech, Cape Town, 9 February 1996; OAU Summit speech, Yaounde, 8 July 1996; Freedom of the City of London, Guildhall speech, 10 July 1996; joint Houses of Parliament speech, London, 11 July 1996; Bastille Day speech, Paris, 14 July 1996;

Warrenton Presidential School Project speech, 30 August 1996; signing of the South African constitution speech, Sharpeville, 10 December 1996; Food for Life, Pietermaritzburg speech, 23 April 1997; Freedom of Pietermaritzburg speech, 25 April 1997; Lecture at the Oxford Centre for Islamic Studies, 11 July 1997.